HIDE TO SURVIVE!

Animal Camouflage in the OCEAN

by Ruth Owen

Ruby Tuesday BOOKS

Published in 2024 by Ruby Tuesday Books Ltd.

Copyright © 2024 Ruby Tuesday Books Ltd.

Editor: Mark J. Sachner
Design & Production: Tammy West

Photo credits:
Nature Picture Library: 4 (Alex Mustard), 13 (Juergen Freund), 15 (Shane Gross), 17 (Georgette Douwma), 19 (Norbert Wu); Shutterstock: Cover (Timothy Baxter), 1 (beara creative), 5 (Gerald Robert Fischer), 7 (Martin Prochazkacz), 8–9 (kaschibo), 11 (John A. Andersen), 21 (mobrafotografie), 21 (Michael Warwick), 22B (tank200bar), 23 (Fotokon).

Library of Congress Control Number: 2023950845

Print (Hardback) ISBN 978-1-78856-385-7
Print (Paperback) ISBN 978-1-78856-386-4
ePub ISBN 978-1-78856-388-8

Published in Minneapolis, MN
Printed in the United States

www.rubytuesdaybooks.com

Contents

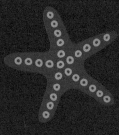

Ocean Hide-and-Seek

How do ocean animals keep safe from **predators** that want to eat them?

Some swim away quickly!

The animals in this book use **camouflage** to blend into their **habitat**.

ghost goby fish

coral polyps

Coral polyps are tiny animals that live in big groups.

Some animals that use camouflage are hunters.

They use camouflage to trick their **prey**.

Can you spot a hunter hiding in the sand?

Will you spot the camouflaged animals in this book?
(You can see where they are hiding on pages 20–21.)

Predator and Prey!

A scorpionfish hides on rocks and **coral reefs**.

Its colors and bumpy skin help it hide.

When a smaller fish passes by, the scorpionfish sucks its prey into its big mouth!

A scorpionfish's camouflage also keeps it safe from sharks and other bigger fish.

Find the Frogfish

Some frogfish change their color to hide from their prey.

They can also change the **texture** of their skin.

Smaller fish and crabs don't spot the hungry frogfish until it's too late!

It takes about two weeks for a frogfish to change color.

coral

Can You See Me in the Sea?

A **pygmy** seahorse is a type of tiny fish.

It lives on coral in the ocean.

It holds on to the coral with its bendy tail.

An adult pygmy seahorse is about half an inch (1.5 cm) long.

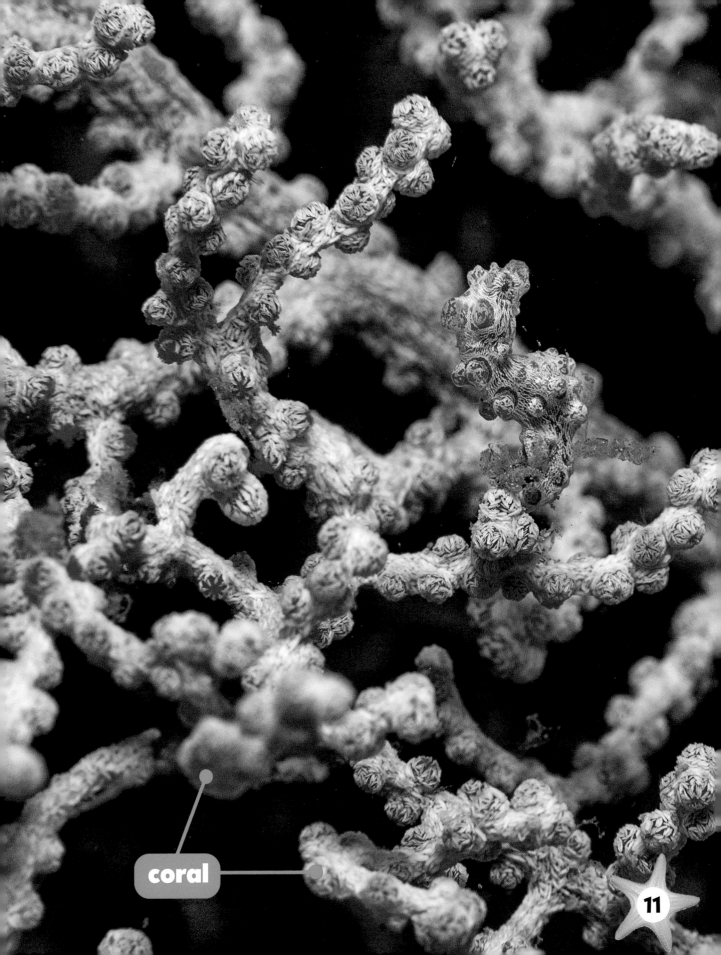

coral

Cucumber Hide-and-Seek

A tiny emperor shrimp keeps safe from its predators by hiding on a neighbor.

It lives on an animal called a sea cucumber.

The shrimp eats little animals and tiny bits of seaweed that stick to the sea cucumber's body.

As the sea cucumber moves from place to place, the shrimp goes, too!

This is a close-up picture of a sea cucumber's body.

Lots of Legs to Hide!

An octopus can blend into its background in seconds.

It changes the color of its skin.

It can also make its skin look bumpy or spiky, like rough rocks or coral.

An octopus hides to keep its soft body safe from hungry sharks.

Cotton Candy Hide-and-Seek

A tiny, pink candy crab lives on corals that are called cotton candy corals.

It uses its grabbing claws to put corals onto its body.

The tiny corals live on the crab and make its camouflage even better!

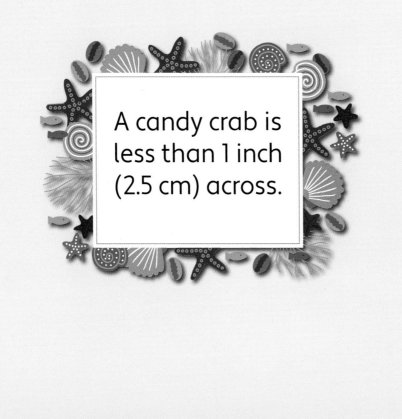

A candy crab is less than 1 inch (2.5 cm) across.

cotton candy
corals

A Leafy Seadragon

A leafy seadragon is a small fish.

It has body parts made of skin that look like floating seaweed.

Its leafy camouflage helps it hide from bigger fish in seaweed.

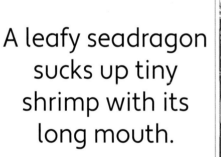

A leafy seadragon sucks up tiny shrimp with its long mouth.

Did You Spot Them?

5   stargazer fish

eye

teeth

This hunter hides from its prey in sand.

7

scorpionfish

9

frogfish

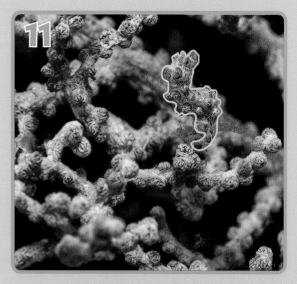

11

pygmy seahorse

emperor shrimp

13

sea cucumber

15

eye

leg

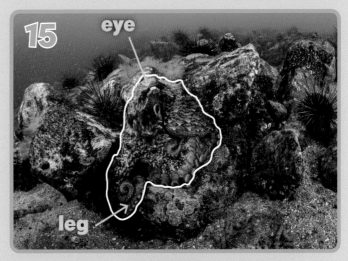

octopus

17

candy crab

head

19

leafy seadragon

21

Glossary

camouflage

Colors, markings, or body parts that help an animal blend into its habitat.

scorpionfish

coral

A tiny ocean animal. Some corals grow hard shells that join together and look like rock.

coral reef

A rocky place made from the hard shells of many tiny corals.

habitat

The place where a living thing makes its home.

predator

An animal that hunts and eats other animals.

prey

An animal that is hunted by other animals for food.

pygmy

Smaller than normal.

texture

How something feels—for example, bumpy or smooth.

Index

Read More

Owen, Ruth. *In Disguise: How Animals Hide from Predators* (*Tell Me More! Science*). Minneapolis, MN: Ruby Tuesday Books (2021).

Wood, Alix. *Welcome to the Ocean. (Nature's Neighborhoods: All About Ecosystems).* Minneapolis, MN: Ruby Tuesday Books (2024).